Collins

Primary Social Studies for Antigua and Barbuda

STUDENT'S BOOK
GRADE 1

Anthea S Thomas

William Collins' dream of knowledge for all began with the publication of his first book in 1819.
A self-educated mill worker, he not only enriched millions of lives, but also founded a flourishing publishing house. Today, staying true to this spirit, Collins books are packed with inspiration, innovation and practical expertise. They place you at the centre of a world of possibility and give you exactly what you need to explore it.

Collins. Freedom to teach.

Published by Collins
An imprint of HarperCollins*Publishers*
The News Building
1 London Bridge Street
London SE1 9GF

HarperCollins*Publishers*
Macken House, 39/40 Mayor Street Upper,
Dublin 1, D01 C9W8, Ireland

Browse the complete Collins Caribbean catalogue at
www.collins.co.uk/caribbeanschools

© HarperCollins*Publishers* Limited 2020
Maps © Collins Bartholomew Limited 2020, unless otherwise stated

10 9 8 7 6 5 4 3

ISBN 978-0-00-840284-6

British Library Cataloguing-in-Publication Data
A catalogue record for this publication is available from the British Library.

Author: Anthea S. Thomas
Publisher: Elaine Higgleton
In-house senior editor: Julianna Dunn
Development & copy editor: Sue Chapple
Proof reader: Mitch Fitton
Cover designers: Kevin Robbins and Gordon MacGilp
Cover image: Steve Evans
Typesetter: QBS
Illustrator: Danielle Boodoo-Fortuné
Production controller: Lyndsey Rogers
Printed and Bound in the UK using 100% Renewable Electricity at CPI Group (UK) Ltd

The publishers gratefully acknowledge the permission granted to reproduce the copyright material in this book. Every effort has been made to trace copyright holders and to obtain their permission for the use of copyright material. The publishers will gladly receive any information enabling them to rectify any error or omission at the first opportunity.

Acknowledgements

The publishers wish to thank the following for permission to reproduce photographs. Every effort has been made to trace copyright holders and to obtain their permission for the use of copyright materials. The publishers will gladly receive any information enabling them to rectify any error or omission at the first opportunity.
(t = top, c = centre, b = bottom, l = left, r = right)

p8tl: Rawpixel.com/SS, p8tr: Greatstock / Alamy Stock Photo, p8b: oliveromg/SS, p10: Shutterstock, p11t: Imfoto/SS, p11b: Shutterstock, p13tl: Leonard Zhukovsky/SS, p13tr: Keith Larby / Alamy Stock Photo, p13b: Mark Summerfield / Alamy Stock Photo, p16: ZUMA Press Inc / Alamy Stock Photo, p17t: Bash Mutumba/SS, p17c: catalin eremia/SS, p17b: margouillat photo/SS, p18t: Lux Blue/SS, p18b: byvalet/SS, p19: DiversityStudio/SS, p20: In The Light Photography/SS, p21t: chromoprisme/SS, p21b: Thoom/SS, p22l: Mark Summerfield / Alamy Stock Photo, p22r: Image Professionals GmbH / Alamy Stock Photo, p23: vladm/SS, p24t: Sibrikov Valery/SS, p24bl: Barbara Ash/SS, p24br: Idea tank/SS, p25t: Anton Starikov/SS, p25bl: He2/SS, p25br: studiolab/SS, p26: Eightshot_Studio/SS, p27: Julinzy/SS, p29t: Prachaya Roekdeethaweesab/SS, p29b: Gary Blake / Alamy Stock Photo, p30tl: Editor's own, p30tc: XiXinXing/SS, p30tr: michaeljung/SS, p30bl: Shutterstock, p30br: Jacob Lund/SS, p32tl: Visual Generation/SS, p32tr: Ekaterina_Mikhaylova/SS, p32cl: VectorsMarket/SS, p32cr: HappyPictures/SS, p32b: Art studio G/SS, p33t: agefotostock / Alamy Stock Photo, p33b: mavo/SS, p34tl: Dave Pot/SS, p34tr: Kanyapak Lim/SS, p34cl: 1EYEman/SS, p34cr: ANEK SANGKAMANEE/SS, p34b: mauritius images GmbH / Alamy Stock Photo, p35t: Dennis MacDonald / Alamy Stock Photo, p35c: Jennifer Chamblee/SS, p35b: Slick Shoots / Alamy Stock Photo, p36t: Tupungato/SS, p36c: Svetlana Shamshurina/SS, p36b: NuN547/SS, p37t: Geir Olav Lyngfjell/SS, p37b: National Geographic Image Collection / Alamy Stock Photo, p38: Gordon Mills / Alamy Stock Photo, p39: Anton_Medvedev/SS, p40tl: CLIPAREA l Custom media/SS, p40tr: nevodka/SS, p40b: Photographee.eu/SS, p41l: Mike Kipling Photography / Alamy Stock Photo, p41r: Minerva Studio/SS, p42t: Tommy E Trenchard / Alamy Stock Photo, p42b: Apple White / Alamy Stock Photo, p43: Zabavna/SS, p44: ClickAlps Srls / Alamy Stock Photo, p45: Hemis / Alamy Stock Photo, p47t: Rawpixel.com/SS, p47b: Rawpixel.com/SS, p48: Aquir/SS, p49: Editor's own, p50l: tommaso79/SS, p50r: PhotoRR/SS, p51: Binkski/SS, p52: Charles O. Cecil / Alamy Stock Photo, p53: 2xSamara.com/SS, p54l: Carsten Reisinger/SS, p54tc: Butterfly Hunter/SS, p54tr: Vitezslav Valka/SS, p54cl: Zoart Studio/SS, p54cr: quantx/SS, p54 bl: Pavlo S/SS, p54br: Kamilon/SS, p55t: Antigua and Barbuda Road Safety Group Inc., p55b: Antigua and Barbuda Transport Board, p56: Richard Cummins / Alamy Stock Photo/SS, p59: beach rob / Alamy Stock Photo, p60t: Graham Prentice / Alamy Stock Photo, p60b: ATGImages / Alamy Stock Photo, p61: EQRoy/SS, p62t: byvalet/SS, p62b: Art Directors & TRIP / Alamy Stock Photo, p63: Marzolino/SS, p64: SH-Vector/SS, p65tl: wavebreakmedia/SS, p65tr: Andrey_Popov/SS, p65bl: Anatoliy Karlyuk/SS, p65br: Andrey_Popov/SS, p67tl: Leszek Kobusinski/SS, p67tc: NEGOVURA/SS, p67tr: DONOT6_STUDIO/SS, p67bl: Oleksiy Mark/SS, p67br: M.Stasy/SS, p68t: Editor's own, p68b: Oleksiy Mark/SS, p69t: Editor's own, p69b: JocularityArt/SS, p70t: Editor's own, p70b: Editor's own, p71t: Fleur_de_papier/SS, p71b: Dragos Dragomirescu/SS.

Contents

1 All about me

We are learning to:

- give our names, describe ourselves and our feelings
- understand the basic rights of a child
- describe our families
- say how families can get bigger or smaller
- say things we do to help at home
- describe our neighbourhood
- find our homes on a map of our neighbourhood
- find Antigua on a map of the Caribbean.

Who am I?

When you were born, your parents gave you a special name. Each of us has a special name. It helps to identify us.

This is Kimmie.
She is a girl.

This is Jerel.
He is a boy.

What do I look like?

In Kindergarten, you learned the names for parts of the body. You can use these words to say what you look like.

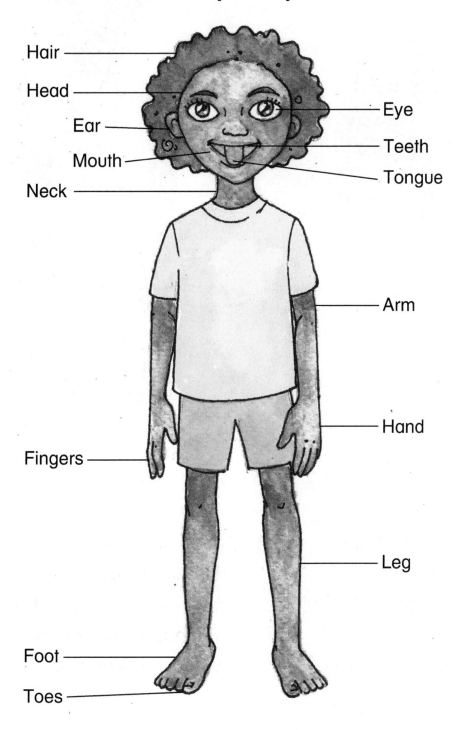

Here are Kimmie and Jerel again.

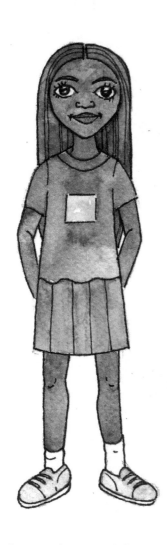

Kimmie is a short girl.
She is slim.
She has long hair. It is black.
She has brown eyes.
She has a broad nose.
She has a small mouth.

Jerel is a tall boy.
He is strong.
He has short hair. It is brown.
He has brown eyes.
He has a slim nose.
He has a broad mouth

What do I do?

You can talk about the things that you do, to describe yourself.

Nathan shares his lunch with his classmates. He is kind.

Kimmie likes to help her mother. She is a helpful girl.

Here are some other words we can use to describe ourselves:

> funny   happy   smart   caring   friendly

When we can do things for ourselves, we usually feel good.
For example:

John is happy that he can tie his shoelaces.

Stacey is happy that she can catch a ball.

Keneil is happy that he can play football and cricket.

The rights of a child

As a child, you have some basic rights, by law.
These include:

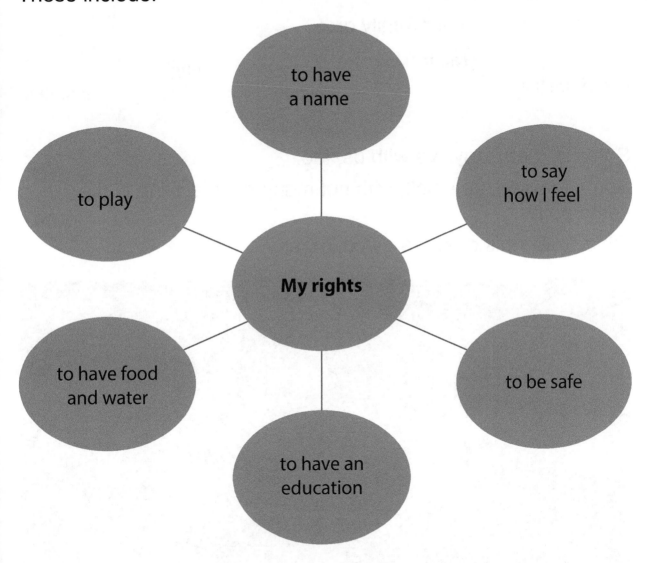

to have a name

to say how I feel

to play

My rights

to have food and water

to be safe

to have an education

My family

Our parents, brothers, sisters, and so on, are our family. We usually live with them.

Other members of our family are:

grandfather

uncles

grandmother

aunts

cousins

Some of them may live with us, too.

Some families are small, with not many people living in the same home.

Others, like this one, are much larger.

Families don't stay the same. They get bigger or smaller.

Families get smaller when someone dies or when an adult moves away to live somewhere else.

Families get bigger when a baby is born, or when new adults move in.

Playing your part at home

Members of a family help each other. They work together and they play together.

There are lots of ways you can help at home, too. You can help by:

- keeping your room clean
- putting your toys away when you stop playing with them
- taking out the garbage
- helping when someone is sick.

A neighbourhood

Families living close together make up a neighbourhood.
A neighbourhood can be small or big.

Besides our homes, our neighbourhood has some other
important places, as you can see here.

Some bigger neighbourhoods have other important places, like ...

... an airport

... a bank

... a hospital.

A community

A group of neighbourhoods make up a community. A community may also be called a village.

There are several villages in Antigua and Barbuda. You can see some of them on this map.

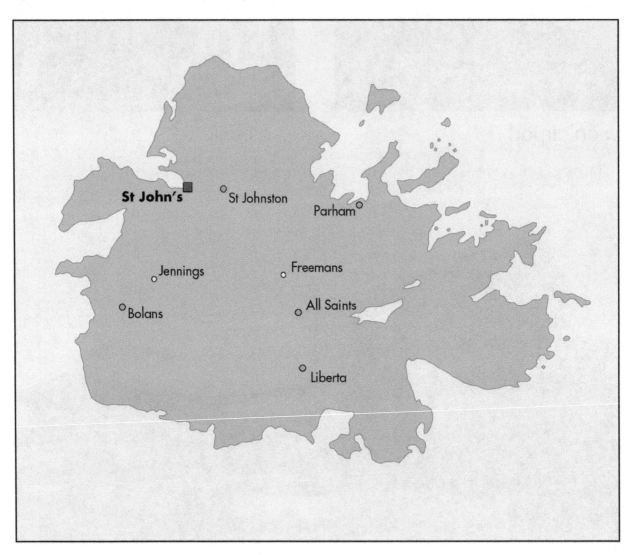

This map shows where Antigua and Barbuda is, in the Eastern Caribbean.

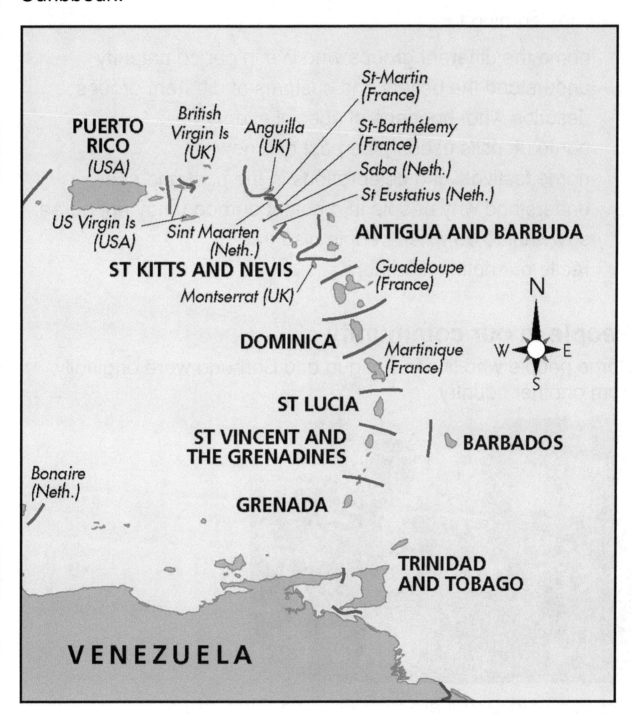

2 Our culture

We are learning to:

- name the different groups who live in our community
- understand the beliefs and customs of different groups
- describe what happens at special events
- name utensils used in the past and now
- name festivals and celebrations in the past and now
- understand why people in a neighbourhood may not agree
- say what to do when people disagree
- recite our national anthem.

People in our community

Some people who live in Antigua and Barbuda were originally from another country.

Sandy's neighbours are from Guyana. They are called Guyanese people. They like to cook food with curry spices.

Nathan's neighbours are from Jamaica.
They are called Jamaicans.
They love reggae music.

There is a shawarma shop next to Shane's house. The people who own it are from Syria. They are called Syrians. They sell chicken shawarma, and sometimes pizza, too.

There are lots of Chinese shops in our communities. The people who own them came originally from China. They like to sell chicken and fried rice.

People who come from different countries do some things differently from us. Their way of life is called their **culture**.

Culture includes how we dress, dance, speak and cook food, as well as our religious beliefs and the music we listen to. We can really enjoy these differences, seeing what life is like in other cultures.

Families in the neighbourhood have different religious beliefs. They worship differently and on different days. Some people go to church on Sundays while some go to church on Saturdays.

Family traditions

Families have traditions. These are things that they always do, like going on a picnic on Easter Monday or having a special meal on birthdays.

Church ceremonies

Many family traditions involve the church.

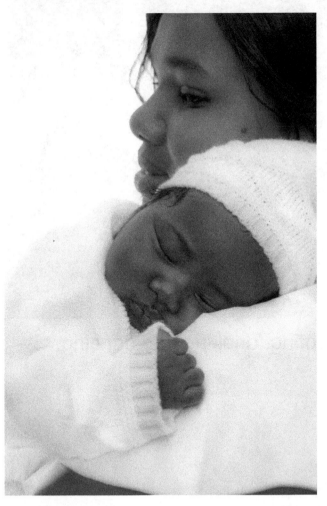

Some families have a baby dedication, a few weeks after a baby has been born. This is where the baby is taken to church and everyone prays to dedicate the baby to God. It is a happy tradition.

Another happy occasion is when two people get married. This is often at a church. Family members and friends are invited to the ceremony.

Later, there is a reception with eating, drinking and dancing.

When someone in the community dies, there is a funeral service. This is where people gather, usually at the church, to say things about the person who died before they are buried. It is a sad occasion and many people cry.

Another church ceremony is a **confirmation**. This is for children who want to become members of a Christian church. The children usually wear white at the ceremony.

Community celebrations

Popular celebrations and festivals in Antigua and Barbuda include Carnival, Sailing Week, Christmas, Easter and Independence. People from around the country come together to enjoy these celebrations.

Christmas

Carnival

Sometimes new celebrations become part of our tradition.

There is one celebration that used to be very popular in the past but is not really celebrated any more. This is Guy Fawkes Night.

This celebration came from the UK. It was held in November each year. There were always lots of fireworks.

Today, we have more fireworks on New Year's Eve, as we say goodbye to one year and welcome in the next.

Other changes in the way we live

Some things, like Carnival, are old traditions that don't change very much from year to year. In other ways, our way of life can change quite quickly, as new things are invented to make our lives easier.

A good example of this is the tools we have to help us prepare food. These tools are called **utensils**. Here are some examples of utensils past and present.

Many of the utensils that we used in the past, like plates and cups, were made from tin or wood. Some were made from the tins of food products, such as the cheese tin. The calabash was used to make bowls and clay was used to make pots.

Today, most of the utensils we use are made from plastic, stainless steel and glass.

How can we all get along?

In any community, it's very important that people get along with each other. This is true in your school, and for all of us in our neighbourhood – and in the country, too.

Sometimes that isn't easy. Everybody is different and that can bring problems. Children might argue when they are playing a game. Adults might argue about the best way to cook pepperpot, whether it's with meat and vegetables in the traditional Antiguan way, or just with meat, as in Guyana.

The important thing is to accept that different people have different ideas. If we respect that, we will get along with others in our community.

It's also important to behave in the correct way and to obey the rules of our community. For example, if the national anthem is played, we know we should stand to attention. This may be at school, at church, or when watching some sport.

Here is the our national anthem.

Fair Antigua and Barbuda
We thy sons and daughters stand,
Strong and firm in peace or danger
To safeguard our native land.
We commit ourselves to building
A true nation brave and free.
Ever striving ever seeking
Dwell in love and unity.

Raise the standard! Raise it boldly!
Answer now to duty's call
To the service of thy country,
Sparing nothing, giving all;
Gird your loins and join the battle
'Gainst fear, hate and poverty,
Each endeavouring, all achieving,
Live in peace where man is free.

God of nations, let Thy blessings
Fall upon this land of ours;
Rain and sunshine ever sending,
Fill her fields with crops and flowers;
We her children do implore Thee,
Give us strength, faith, loyalty,
Never failing, all enduring
To defend her liberty.

3 What do we need?

Basic needs

We all need certain things in order to survive. These are called our basic needs. Our basic needs are food, shelter, clothing, air and water.

Our parents and other adults in the family work to provide our basic needs. When they work, they get money. This money is used to buy food and clothes, and to buy or build a home.

Some families make some or all of their own food. They grow fruits and vegetables, and may keep animals for eggs, milk and meat.

Workers in the community

Workers do many different jobs to earn money. You can see some of them here. Can you think of any others?

Shopkeeper

Hairdresser

Mechanic

Nurse

Cook

What do they do?

I work in a shop. I sell goods.

I do people's hair, to help them look good!

I look after people who are sick.

I cook food in a restaurant.

I fix cars, vans and buses.

What do they use?

Most workers have to use special tools in order to get their jobs done. They take special care of these tools so that they can last a long time.

A shopkeeper uses a till to keep the money in.

A hairdresser uses scissors when they need to cut hair.

A nurse uses a thermometer to see if someone has a fever.

A cook uses pots and pans to cook food in.

A mechanic uses a spanner – and lots of other tools, too.

Jobs of long ago and jobs of today

Many years ago, a lot of sugar and cotton was grown in Antigua and Barbuda. They were grown on plantations and were sold to countries all around the world.

Many men and women worked on these plantations. They planted and harvested sugar and cotton. Some women worked as housekeepers in the homes of the plantation owners. They were the only jobs people could do. There were hardly any doctors or nurses, no teachers for children, no shops or hairdressers.

Today, sugar and cotton are no longer grown and many people now work in offices. There are plenty of doctors, lawyers, taxi-drivers, teachers and bus drivers.

Natural resources

Resources are things that are useful to us. They include water, plants and trees, animals and land. We use them for many things.

Water

We use water in many different ways. Mostly we use fresh water.

We use it for drinking.

We use it for cooking.

We use it for washing.

Farmers use it to water their plants.

The water in the sea is salt water. We can't drink it, but we can eat the fish who live in it.

And we enjoy swimming and playing in it!

Land

We use land to grow vegetables and crops for food.

We use land for building homes, schools, shops, churches, hospitals – and playgrounds, too.

We use land to build roads, to help us travel around.

Plants and trees

We use trees and plants to give us fruit and vegetables to eat. Plants give us food for animals, too.

Trees give us wood that we can use for building. We can make paper from the wood, too.

Trees give us shade from the hot sun.

We can get medicine from plants as well, to help us get better when we are sick. And some animals use trees and plants as their homes.

Animals

A lot of our food comes from animals.

Animals like dogs and cats can be pets, or some animals can keep our homes safe from robbers.

In the past, we used animals like donkeys for transport. In colder countries, the wool from sheep is used for wool, to make warm clothes.

People

People are one of the most important resources a country can have. They have the knowledge and skills needed to use all the other resources.

Goods and services

People use the resources around them to produce goods and to provide a service for other people.

Goods

Goods are things that we buy and sell. They are things that we can touch. We use the money that we earn from our work, to buy things. For example, when we want food we go to the supermarket, give money to the shop and receive the food in exchange.

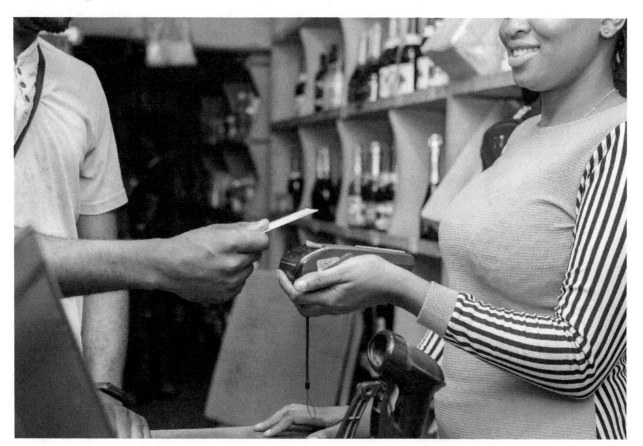

Here are some examples of goods that we can buy. There are many more, like shoes, clothes and toys.

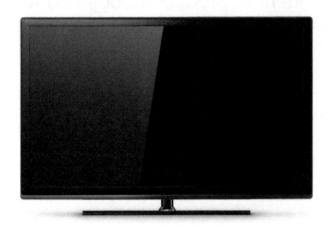

Services

Some people do not produce goods but they provide a service. A service is useful work done to help other people. We can't touch services.

The people who provide a service receive money in return. For example:

- You pay a taxi driver to take you where you want to go.
- When you are sick you pay a doctor to tell you what you need to do to get well, and to give you some medicine.
- A policeman provides a service by protecting us from harm and danger.

Changing landscapes

The land around us is always changing.

The land changes naturally when we have disasters like hurricanes, earthquakes and floods.

An earthquake can cause terrible damage, like here in Haiti.

A hurricane can destroy all our crops.

The land is changed by us when we cut down trees, or clear the land to build houses and to make roads. The more people there are in a country, the more land is needed to build houses.

Trees being felled.

Looking after our community

We live in a beautiful country. If we are not careful, we can destroy our community, by cutting down too many trees and by throwing garbage on the ground and in the water.

If we cut down trees, we need to plant new ones to replace them. We must put our garbage in covered bins and keep our community clean.

4 Leaders

We are learning to:

- name groups we belong to
- name things that different groups do
- say what would happen if groups had no leader
- name various leaders in Antigua and Barbuda
- understand the responsibilities of leaders
- say what can happen if rules are not followed
- understand the correct behaviour in school activities.

Being part of a group

A group is a set of people who do similar things. We all belong to one or more groups – a family group, for example.

Other groups that we may be a part of include church, choir, class, school, football, cricket, dance, the Girls' Brigade and the Boy Scouts.

Some groups are just for having fun and meeting people, while others also teach us how to do things:

- We learn to dance in a dance group.
- We learn to play football at a football club.
- We learn to sing in a choir.
- We get an education at school.

We also learn how to get along with other people when we are part of a group. We have rules to follow so that the group works well, and we find out that we can do more things and do them better when we are part of a team.

There are much bigger groups in the country, too. Even the government has to work together as a group.

Leaders

Each group has a leader. The leader is someone who makes sure that the members of the group work together to do the things that they need to do.

- Your parents are the leaders of your family.
- A principal is the leader of a school.
- A teacher is the leader of a class.
- A pastor is the leader of a church.
- A prime minister is the leader of a country.

In some groups the leader is called a president. For example, the leader of the Parent Teachers Association is called the president.

Some important leaders in Antigua and Barbuda include:
- The Governor General
- The Prime Minister
- The Leader of the Opposition

What if we had no leaders?

What would happen if there were no leaders? There would be no order. Everyone would want to do as they please. Children would go to school when they felt like it and would not listen to their parents.

Responsibilities of leaders

Leaders make sure that everything is organised. They encourage members of their group to do their best and to work together. They make sure that the rules are followed. They make decisions and they appoint other people to do things.

Rules

Rules are special instructions that tells us how to behave. Most groups have rules.

Families have rules for how children should behave. These might be the chores they need to do, the time they need to go to bed, or how much time they can spend watching TV, for example.

Schools have rules to make sure children learn and that they are kept safe.

When rules are not followed, there are consequences. For example, at school you should not be out of class without your teacher's permission. If you are caught doing this, you will be punished.

We should always obey the rules of the groups we are in. Many of the rules are there to keep us safe. For example, you are told not to play with matches so that you won't get burnt.

School rules

Some school rules are there to make sure the school runs well and children learn as much as they can. These are rules like:

- Arrive at school on time.
- Do all your homework and hand it in on time.
- Don't cheat in a test.
- Don't run inside the school.

Other rules are more about how to behave towards other people.

These rules are about showing respect to other people. They are good rules to follow right through life.

5 Safety

We are learning to:

- name rules children should follow to stay safe when travelling
- understand the importance of traffic signs
- show the correct use of road signs and notices
- name groups and organisations that have road safety programmes
- say how they help to keep children safe.

Safety rules

In the previous unit you learned about rules in groups. There are also rules to make sure we are safe when we are travelling. Obeying the rules keeps us safe from accidents. Many people are injured or die in road accidents because they don't obey the safety rules.

Rules for travelling on foot

Before you cross the road, check carefully for any cars coming. In Antigua, because we drive on the left-hand side of the road, you must look right, then left, then right again.

- If you are at a traffic light, wait for the green 'walk' sign before you step out.
- Use a pedestrian crossing if there is one.
- Walk at the side of the road unless you are crossing to the other side.
- Walk facing the traffic coming towards you.

Rules for travelling in a car

- Wear your seatbelt at all times.
- Don't hang your head, hands, or any other part of your body out of the window.
- Don't make a lot of noise because it can disturb the driver.
- Sit down at all times.

Rules when playing

- Don't play near the road.
- If a ball you're playing with goes into the road, don't just run after it. Stop, and obey all the rules for the road.
- Play fairly.
- Don't push anyone.

Traffic signs

There are many traffic signs and signals all around the country. These signs tell drivers and pedestrians what they should do.

Obeying the traffic signs stops many accidents. Here are some of the common signs. Do you know what they all mean?

Road safety organisations

Road safety is so important that there are special organisations to help us. For example, the Antigua and Barbuda Road Safety Group tells drivers what they must do – and what they mustn't do – in order to prevent road accidents. They put signs up across the country, like these.

The Antigua and Barbuda Transportion Board makes sure that all the road signs are put in the right place and that the roads are marked clearly.

6 Moving about

We are learning to:

- name places people travel to in the neighbourhood
- use directions to give the location of places
- name the points on the compass and use them to locate places in Antigua and Barbuda
- name the modes of transportation and transportation centres
- say which types of transportation would be used to go to different places
- say what life would be like without transport.

Where do we go?

Every day we move from place to place in our neighbourhood. We go to school, church, shops, the supermarket, the cinema and the playground. Adults go to work. This movement is called travelling.

Using a map

A map is a drawing of an area. It will usually show the main places in that area. We can say where these places are on the map by using words such as 'up', 'down', 'left' and 'right'.

Look at this map of a neighbourhood. We can say that the school is left of the church. The playground is down from the school and the shop is near to the church.

We can also use the points of a compass to say where a place is. You can see the compass on the map above. It shows the points North, South, West and East.

Look at this map of Antigua from Unit 1. Using a compass, we can see that All Saints is north of Liberta, and Bolans is south of Jennings.

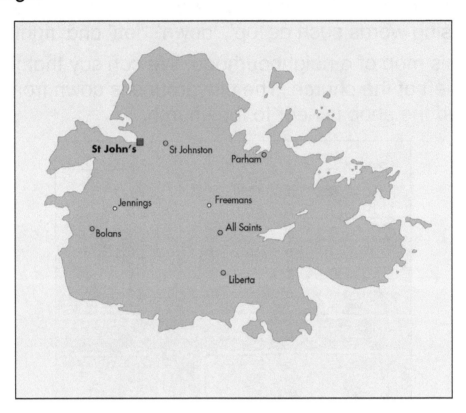

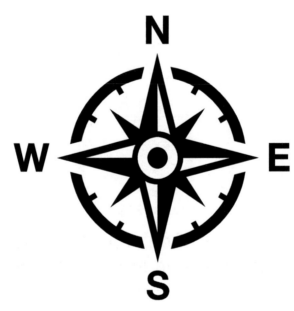

Transportation

We don't walk everywhere we want to go. We use a form of transportation. There are three main types of transportation: land, sea and air.

Land transportation

This photo, taken in St John's, shows many examples of land transportation, including cars, buses and motor cycles.

Other examples include trucks, bicycles, tractors, ambulances and fire engines. Trains also travel on land, although we don't have trains in our country.

Sea transportation

We use the sea to transport people and goods to other countries. Examples include boats, yachts, cruise ships, cargo ships and ferries.

The country of Antigua and Barbuda is made up of two islands. We use a ferry to travel between the two islands. This ferry is in St John's and is waiting to take people to Barbuda.

Ferries also carry people and goods between Antigua and many other Caribbean islands.

Air transportation

Air transportation is the fastest of all. It is mostly used to travel between countries. Examples include airplanes, helicopters and hot air balloons.

We choose a different type of transportation depending on where we want to go.

- To go somewhere nearby, if we don't want to walk, we will go by bicycle.
- To go to a supermarket that is far away, or if we are buying a lot of shopping, we will go by car.
- A person who doesn't drive a car will use a bus to take them into town or to work.
- To go to another island, or another country, we will go by sea.
- If we need to get to another island or country more quickly, we will go by air.

Transportation centres

If we are using public transport, we need to go to a transportation centre.

The international **airport** is the transportation centre we go to when we want to travel by air.

If we want to travel by air, we go to the international airport in St John's.

We need to go to the **harbour** if we want to travel by sea. There are several habours around Antigua and Barbuda.

St John's Harbour is the main harbour for passengers.

The **bus station** is the place you go to when you want to travel by bus. There are two bus stations in Antigua and Barbuda.

This is the West Bus Station in St John's. Buses from here go the west part of the island.

Travelling in the past

Long ago, there were no cars, buses, airplanes or ships to get us to places. It took a long time to get to anywhere that wasn't just nearby.

Imagine walking to your school from Newfield, or walking into town from Old Road.

Old Road is very long!

7 Communication

We are learning to:

- say what it means to communicate
- understand why people need to communicate
- name instruments used for communicating
- understand methods of communication
- name communication centres
- name workers in the community who are communication workers.

What is communication?

Kenya told his mother he was feeling sick.

Shania held up six fingers when her teacher asked her how old she was.

Kenya and Shania are **communicating**.

When we communicate we are sending and receiving messages. We communicate every day to show how we feel, to share our ideas and to give information to other people.

Here you can see some of the reasons why we communicate.

To make friends

To ask for help, or to offer help

To say you're sad or happy

Why do we communicate?

To make people smile and laugh

To say you're hungry or thirsty

Mostly, we communicate by talking. We can also communicate using:

- signs
- symbols
- paintings or other pictures
- body language such as smiling, frowning, shrugging our shoulders.

We can use different instruments to help us communicate.

Telephone

Letter

Newspaper

Radio

Computer

Communication centres

There are special places that help us to send and receive messages. These are called communication centres.

The post office

Letters that we send to other people and that other people send to us, go through the post office.

This is the main post office in St John's. There are smaller post offices in towns and villages around the country.

Media houses

Radio stations, television stations and newspapers provide a way for us to communicate by receiving their messages. It is how we find out what is going on in our country

Telecom companies

Telecom companies like Flow, Digicel and APUA provide us with the signals we need to send and receive messages using landline phones, mobile phones and televisions.

Communications workers

Many of the people who work for our community are communications workers.

We often see the postman or postwoman, who goes from door to door to deliver the mail that has been sent to us.

All these photos show examples of communication that workers have created and put in place for us They give us important information that we need to know. Others are adverts trying to persuade us to buy something, or to welcome visitors to our country!

Departures ✈

Time	Destination	Flight	Gate	Status
12:00	Hong-Kong	HK4701	A56	Boarding
12:03	London	HT964	D15	Delayed
12:03	New York	HK4701	B56	Boarding
12:12	Amsterdam	HK487	C12	Cancelled
12:25	Buenos Aires	BA2578	B6	Boarding
12:26	Dusseldorf	DS4307	E4	Boarding
12:40	Oslo	OS258	B10	Boarding
12:55	Dubai	DB1234	C31	Boarding
13:03	Bologna	BL9875	A4	Boarding

Welcome to

ANTIGUA AND BARBUDA